DOWN IN THE OCEAN

CORAL REEF COMMUNITIES

BY MELISSA GISH

CREATIVE EDUCATION • CREATIVE PAPERBACKS

Published by Creative Education and Creative Paperbacks
P.O. Box 227, Mankato, Minnesota 56002
Creative Education and Creative Paperbacks are imprints of
The Creative Company
www.thecreativecompany.us

Design, production, and illustrations by Chelsey Luther
Art direction by Rita Marshall
Printed in China

Photographs by Alamy (Reinhard Dirscherl, David Fleetham, LITTLE DINO-
SAUR, Nature Picture Library, Marli Wakeling, WaterFrame), All-free-download.
com, Dreamstime (Grafner, Jolanta Wojcicka), Getty Images (Reinhard Dirscherl/
WaterFrame, Tim Laman/National Geographic, Tom Meyer/Moment, Carrie Von-
derhaar/Ocean Futures Society/National Geographic), iStockphoto (atese, prasit
chansarekorn, inusuke, miblue5, strmko, ultramarinfoto), Minden Pictures (Jurgen
Freund/NPL), National Geographic Creative (David Doubilet, Stocktrek Images),
Shutterstock (cbpix, Ethan Daniels, Kim David, Vladislav Gajic, J'nel, Lotus_stu-
dio, Strilets, Studio Barcelona)

Library of Congress Cataloging-in-Publication Data
Names: Gish, Melissa, author.
Title: Coral reef communities / Melissa Gish.
Series: Down in the ocean.
Includes bibliographical references and index.
Summary: Explore the regions of the world's oceans known for their coral reefs and
learn about the life forms that dwell there. First-person accounts from scientists an-
swer important questions about reef communities.
Identifiers: LCCN 2017027661 / ISBN 978-1-60818-995-3 (hardcover) / ISBN 978-
1-62832-550-8 (pbk) / ISBN 978-1-64000-024-7 (eBook)

Subjects: LCSH: 1. Coral reef ecology—Juvenile literature. 2. Coral reef animals—
Juvenile literature.
Classification: LCC QH541.5.C7 G57 2018 / DDC 577.7/89—dc23

CCSS: RI.4.1, 2, 7; RI.5.1, 2, 3, 8; RST.6-8.1, 2, 5, 6, 8

First Edition HC 9 8 7 6 5 4 3 2 1
First Edition PBK 9 8 7 6 5 4 3 2 1

TABLE OF CONTENTS

WELCOME TO THE CORAL REEF

Coral reefs cover less than 0.1 percent of the earth. Yet a quarter of all sea life depends on these habitats. Animals that live in the open sea, such as sea turtles and manta rays, sometimes visit coral reefs. But many of the most amazing animals on the planet call coral reefs their home.

Animals that are part of coral reef communities are called residents. There are thousands of resident **species**. Some are big fish. Others are small plants. Also, millions of creatures called plankton drift in the water around a reef. Most are so tiny they can only be seen under a microscope. Every plant and animal has an important role in the coral reef's **ecosystem**.

EARTH'S SURFACE

CORAL REEFS (0.1%)

TOTAL SEA LIFE

RESIDENT CORAL REEF SPECIES (25%)

INFINITE WONDERS

Coral reefs start with tiny animals called coral polyps. They have soft bodies and finger-like tentacles. They make stony skeletons around their bodies. The polyps attach to rock and then divide to create more polyps. Each one makes a new skeleton. These skeletons join together to form colonies. The colonies grow for hundreds and thousands of years. They join other colonies to make a coral reef.

There are four kinds of coral reefs. Fringing reefs are the most common. They grow along shorelines in shallow water. A barrier reef grows farther from shore. It may reach the water's surface. It forms a barrier that prevents ships from passing over it. Atolls are reefs that form rings around islands. As the islands sink into the ocean, the reefs continue to grow. The country of the Maldives in the Indian Ocean is made up of 26 atolls. Patch reefs are like small underwater islands.

KINDS OF CORAL REEFS

FRINGING REEF   BARRIER REEF   ATOLL   PATCH REEF

What's that coral?

Broccoli coral is named for the vegetable. It is a soft coral, unlike polyps. Broccoli corals grow stiff trunks and slender branches like trees. The branches have tiny spikes that protect the coral from predators.

Rainbow colors

Mandarinfish are vividly colored. Bigger fish can easily see them. But many predators avoid these fish. Mandarinfish do not have scales like other fish. Their bodies are covered with thick, stinky slime. The slime tastes awful. Most predators quickly learn to steer clear of mandarinfish.

ASK A 🐙 SCIENTIST

How do coral reefs grow?

Corals are animals that have a unique relationship with microscopic algae living in their tissues. Corals team up with these algae to use the sun's energy to create food. This process is called photosynthesis. It is similar to the way plants grow. As the corals grow, they spread out or grow toward the sun. By growing, corals create structures that can resemble underwater cities.

— Dr. Brian J. Zgliczynski, Marine Ecologist, University of California, San Diego

broccoli coral

mandarinfish

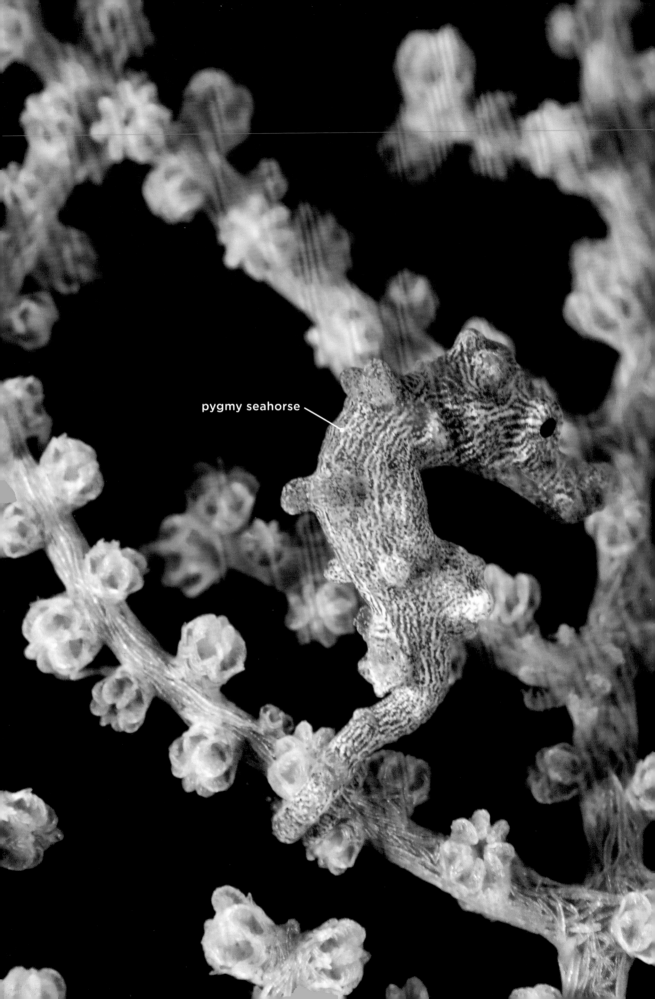

pygmy seahorse

Christmas tree worm

Where's the seahorse?

Pygmy seahorses are hard to find. Their bodies are colored like sea fan corals. This makes the seahorses almost invisible. The Satomi's pygmy seahorse is the world's smallest seahorse. It is half an inch (1.3 cm) long. All other pygmy seahorses are just twice that long.

½ inch

It's a worm!

The Christmas tree worm burrows into the tops of coral reefs. It creates an outer skeleton in the form of a tube. Its frilly tentacles are called radioles. The radioles capture plankton that drifts by. The worm ducks into the tube when predators come around.

13

ASK A 🐙 SCIENTIST

What makes coral reefs unique?

As a group, corals themselves are quite amazing and strange to think about. They live in colonies where there are many, many individuals, but they are all genetic clones of each other. This means they have the same **DNA**. Yet they can function individually and in groups. It is completely unlike the way we, as individual animals, work.

— Dr. James Leichter, Marine Biologist, Scripps Institution of Oceanography

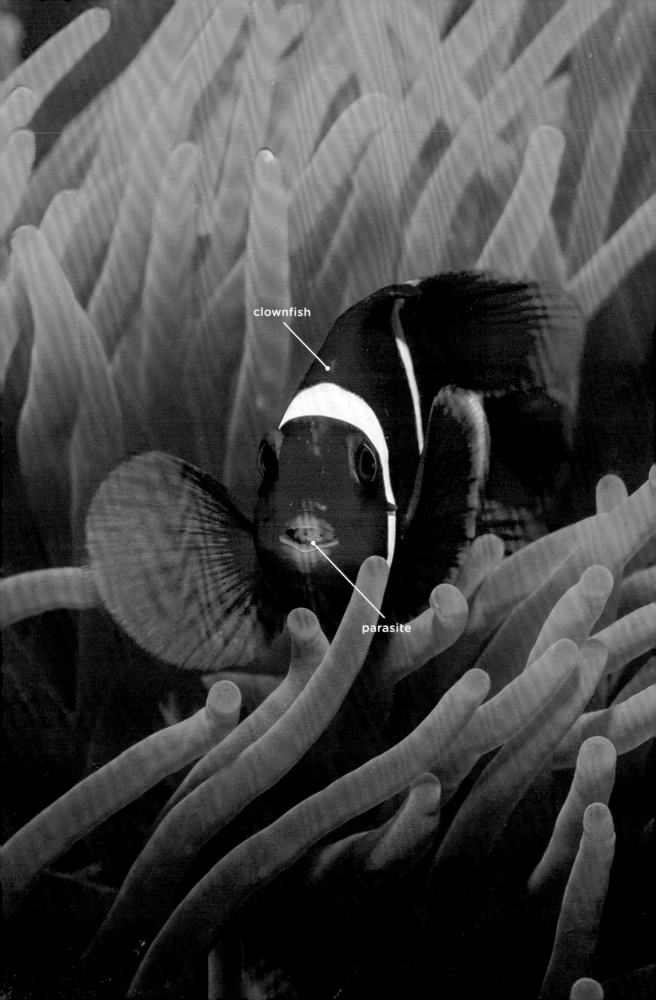

clownfish

parasite

2

EAT OR BE EATEN

Life in the ocean is a constant battle for survival. Some plants are able to make their own food. Many small animals feed on animal waste or dead organisms. Animals that eat plants and algae are called herbivores. Animals that kill other animals to eat are carnivores. Parasites are predators that live on or inside their prey. Their prey is called a host. Parasites may feed on the host. Or they may eat the food their host consumes. Some parasites kill their hosts, but others simply use their hosts.

ANIMAL NUTRITION

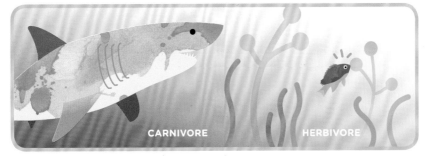

CARNIVORE   HERBIVORE

Fish doctor

The bluestreak cleaner wrasse (*RASS*) is like a fish doctor. It grows to six inches (15.2 cm) in length. Its teeth are like tweezers. It nibbles parasites off other fish. The wrasse even swims inside the mouths of other fish to eat parasites!

Agile imposter

The bluestriped fangblenny is a bold little fish. It pretends to be a cleaner, so larger fish allow it to safely approach. The big fish expects to have parasites nibbled away. Instead, the fangblenny bites chunks of flesh from its victim. Then it quickly darts away.

ASK A 🐙 SCIENTIST

Why aren't coral reefs covered with algae?

Herbivores eat algae. Many guard a small territory. Some herbivore fish can even act as farmers. They weed out **unpalatable** baby algae to farm a lush lawn. This makes the lawn a target for roving fish such as parrotfish, so there is lots of action around their territories. These fish can affect coral reefs because they are known to weed out baby corals, too.

— Dr. David J. Booth, Marine Ecologist, University of Technology Sydney (Australia)

bluestreak cleaner wrasse

bluestriped fangblenny

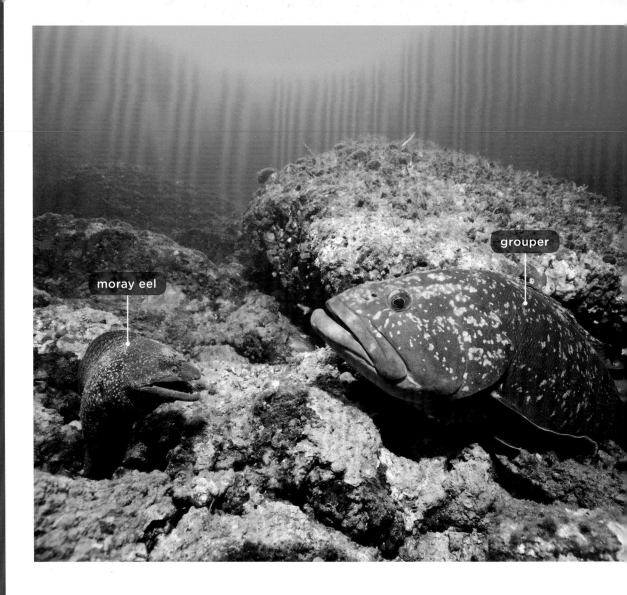

moray eel

grouper

That's teamwork!

Some groupers and moray eels hunt together. When the grouper spots prey in a hiding place, it shakes its body at the moray. This signals the moray to flush out the prey. Then the grouper grabs it. And there's plenty for the moray, too.

butterflyfish

ASK A 🐙 SCIENTIST

How do some fish protect themselves from predators?

Examples are the different species of butterflyfish. Many have developed **adaptations** to help avoid becoming prey. They may blend in with their surroundings or confuse potential predators, such as sharks. Some species have false eyespots near their tails. These make the fish appear to be a larger fish or appear to be facing the opposite direction.

— Dr. Brian J. Zgliczynski, Marine Ecologist, University of California, San Diego

sea cucumber

emperor shrimp

3

SPECIAL RELATIONSHIPS

Having so many creatures crowded into a reef presents challenges. Danger lurks around every corner. The cracks and crevices among corals are important. They provide safe hiding places. But animals cannot hide forever. They need to come out and find food. Many reef animals have adapted by cooperating. They form special relationships. One type of relationship is called mutualism. Partners share their abilities with each other. This arrangement gives something good to both partners. Many coral reef residents have a better chance of survival by working together.

TYPES OF SYMBIOTIC RELATIONSHIPS

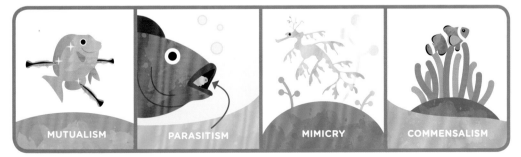

MUTUALISM   PARASITISM   MIMICRY   COMMENSALISM

Sneaky crab

Sponges taste bad or contain poison. Most predators avoid them. Sponge crabs love sponges—not to eat but to wear! They carry sponges on their backs as protection. The sponges win, too. By moving with the crabs, they avoid competing for space on the reef.

Defending each other

At first, sea anemones sting baby clownfish. But then they get used to the fish. They stop stinging. Then the clownfish can safely hide in anemones. They defend anemones from predators such as butterflyfish. Anemones and clownfish even share food!

ASK A 🐙 SCIENTIST

What are sea anemones?

The sea anemone looks like a plant, but it is not. It is an animal. It also looks like a sun, giving rocks pretty colors. Sea anemones eat many different things, including **detritus**. This is important for recycling. They sting when touched. This is to catch small animals to eat. Some fish are safe from their stings. Sea anemones are magical to look at!

— Dr. Dimitri Deheyn, Marine Biologist, Scripps Institution of Oceanography

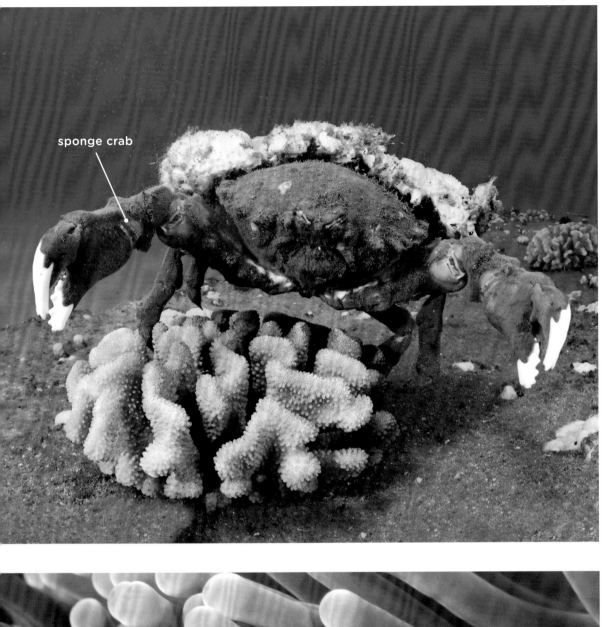

sponge crab

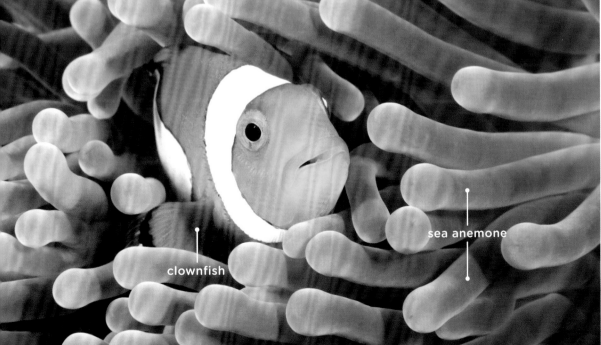

clownfish

sea anemone

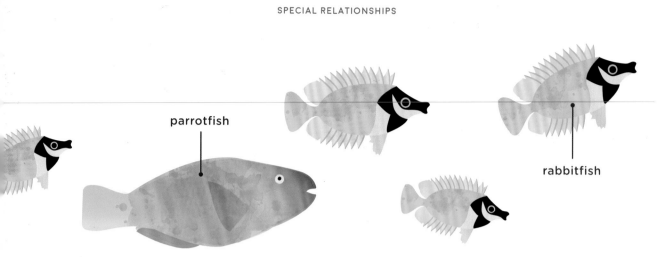

parrotfish

rabbitfish

Fish bodyguards

Parrotfish are slow, defenseless herbivores. Rabbitfish have sharp spines on their fins. Some carry poison. They are well defended against predators. Parrotfish often swim in the middle of rabbitfish schools. When surrounded by these bodyguards, parrotfish can safely travel over the reef.

24

ASK A 🐙 SCIENTIST

Why do large animals sometimes visit coral reefs?

Many kinds of partnerships are found on coral reefs. For example, cleaner shrimp are little red-and-white-striped guys that clean the parasites off larger fish. The shrimp get a meal, and the fish get fewer parasites. Fish and sharks will travel long distances to the same cleaning station to have this service done for them.

— Dr. Rebecca Vega Thurber, Marine Microbiologist, Oregon State University, Corvallis

cleaner shrimp

golden damselfish

4

FAMILY LIFE

Coral reef animals reproduce in different ways. Corals and sponges split and create copies of themselves. Some fish lay eggs that drift away. When the eggs hatch, the young return to the reef. Young cardinal fish find their way home when they are only the size of a pencil eraser. Scientists are not sure how they manage it. Other animals lay eggs that stick to plants and hatch on the reef. Some fish, such as gray reef sharks, give birth to fully formed offspring.

JUVENILE CARDINAL FISH SIZE COMPARISON

This way to the reef! ➔

Devoted father

The seven-figure pygmy goby grows to slightly more than one inch (2.5 cm) long. It has the shortest life span of any vertebrate—just 59 days! In her lifetime, a female may lay up to 400 eggs. Males guard the eggs until they hatch.

1 inch (2.5 cm)

Picking partners

Coral trout begin life as females. Some change to males at four to six years old. To attract a mate, a male coral trout swims around a female. It can darken the color of its fins. This lets the female know that the male is healthy.

ASK A 🐙 SCIENTIST

Is a crowded coral reef unhealthy?

No. For instance, when fish that eat algae are removed from a reef (for example, from overfishing by people), the algae take over. If this happens, corals could disappear. Many of the fish and invertebrates that depend on the corals would decline as well. This happens because every living thing on the reef has **evolved** to fill a role. A crowded reef is actually a healthy reef!

— Dr. Andy Shantz, Ocean Researcher, University of California, Santa Barbara

seven-figure pygmy goby

coral trout

goliath grouper

ASK A 🐙 SCIENTIST

What is the biggest fish on a coral reef?

Goliath groupers can grow to 800 pounds (363 kg) and 9 feet (2.7 m) long. Their eggs are one millimeter in diameter. Baby groupers spend their first six years in **mangrove** forests. When they are about 3 feet long (0.9 m) and about 50 pounds (22.7 kg), they return to the reef. I once saw a goliath grouper eating a green sea turtle. That is one **endangered** species eating another!

— Dr. Christopher Koenig, Reef Fish Ecologist, Florida State University

What a big mouth!

A female yellow-headed jawfish gives her eggs to a male. He carries them in his mouth. He does not eat until they hatch. He protects the eggs from predators. Every so often, he spits them out to clean them. Then he sucks them back in.

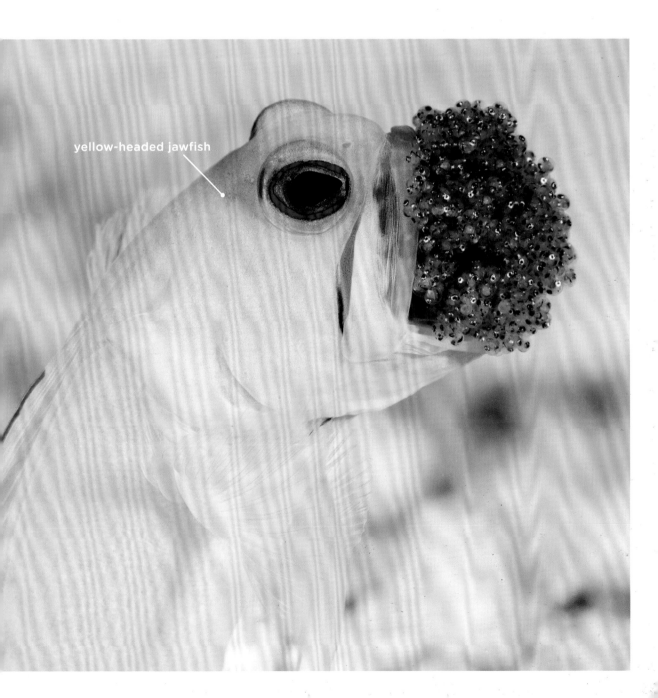

yellow-headed jawfish

5

OCEAN MYSTERIES

Most people see coral reefs in warm, sunny oceans. Reefs usually grow in water that is 150 to 450 feet (45.7–137 m) deep. But coral reefs also exist in places that might seem surprising. In 1982, scientists found a deep-water coral reef in the cold sea off the coast of Norway. In 2010, a deep-sea vessel found a coral reef 2,300 feet (701 m) deep in the Mediterranean Sea off the coast of Israel.

In 2016, scientists in Brazil discovered a coral reef where the Amazon River meets the Atlantic Ocean. The 600-mile-long (966 km) reef is hidden in the muddy, swirling water. Divers found dozens of coral and sponge species. They recorded more than 70 different kinds of fish. We must continue to explore the ocean. Coral reefs still have many mysteries to reveal.

DEPTH ZONES

450 ft .... common reef depth ....

1,776 ft .... One World Trade Center height ....

2,300 ft .... Mediterranean reef depth ....

CONTINENTAL SHELF

Small but powerful

Harlequin shrimp eat only sea stars. A male and female use teamwork to flip sea stars on their backs. Mantis shrimp use their front claws to punch their prey. With the force of a .22 caliber bullet, this punch can shatter crab shells.

Sharks on the reef

Gray reef sharks grow to about five feet (1.5 m) long. Their larger cousins live and hunt in the open sea. But gray reef sharks calmly cruise over the reef. They target sick or weak fish. This behavior keeps the reef healthy.

ASK A SCIENTIST

What is your favorite coral reef fish?

I love all coral reef fish—there are nearly 5,000 species! But I'm a fan of humbug damselfish. They can live in large groups and have complex social behavior. They look out for each other when predators come. But when eating, it's "to each his own." They live in a social structure where "bigger is better." They are hilarious to watch!

— Dr. David J. Booth, Marine Ecologist, University of Technology Sydney (Australia)

mantis shrimp

gray reef shark

reef stonefish

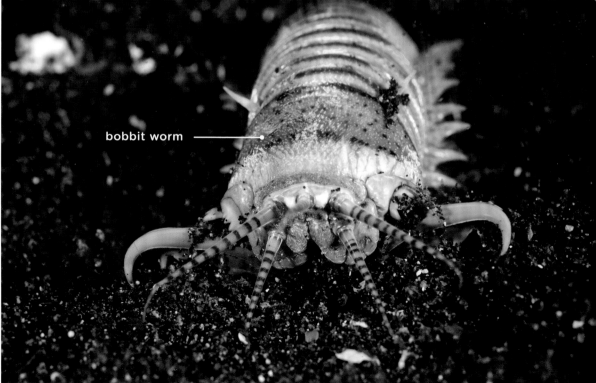

bobbit worm

Deadly disguise

The reef stonefish looks like a rock or stony coral. It grabs fish or crustaceans that pass by. When the stonefish lifts its back fin straight up, watch out! The fin has sharp spines filled with deadly poison that can kill a human.

Hidden trap

Bobbit worms can grow to 10 feet (3 m) long. They hide under the seabed. Their mouths gape open. They can see shadows pass over. When a fish swims overhead, the worm's mouth snaps like a trap. Prey is pulled under the sand.

37

ASK A 🐙 SCIENTIST

What is something new you have learned about coral reefs?

We're learning that the fish that live on coral reefs can also help corals grow. We still don't know exactly how fish do this. One idea is that the extra nutrients in fish "pee" actually act like fertilizer for the algae inside corals. This would allow them to produce more sugar to share with corals and help them grow more quickly.

— Dr. Andy Shantz, Ocean Researcher, University of California, Santa Barbara

TRUE-LIFE CORAL REEF ADVENTURE

DIVING IN THE GREAT BARRIER REEF

Tom Hall grew up in Ohio. When he was five years old, he picked up a library book about Australia. The pictures of kangaroos, koalas, and other strange animals delighted Tom. But when he saw pictures of the Great Barrier Reef, he was captivated. He couldn't believe that such a place existed. He knew at that moment that he wanted to see the Great Barrier Reef with his own eyes!

Years later, Tom traveled to Port Douglas, Australia. His dream was coming true. He was going diving on the Great Barrier Reef! He boarded a boat named *Poseidon*. Tom had never dived before. He needed a quick lesson. A dive instructor named Kane showed Tom how to wear a wetsuit, fins, and weights around his ankles. Weights help divers sink down to the reef. Tom learned how to wear a scuba tank and regulator. The tank carries air to breathe, and the regulator delivers air from the tank into a diver's mouth. When *Poseidon* reached the reef, Tom was ready to dive.

People should never dive alone, so Tom dived with Kane. They slipped into the bright blue water. Kane touched his finger and thumb together, making the "OK" sign with his hand. Tom made the same sign. Tom's signal told Kane that he was ready to go. As he glided over the coral, Tom saw amazing structures of all shapes and sizes. Colorful sponges jutted from ledges, and ribbon eels poked their heads from crevices. Tom spotted a clownfish wriggling through anemone tentacles.

As he turned a corner, he startled a brown-spotted reef cod, which slowly headed the other direction. Two lionfish, guarding their feeding spots, watched Tom swim by. Feather stars waved in the gentle current as a school of striped large-eye bream gracefully passed. A mailed butterflyfish swam through a school of bicolor chromis—small black fish with white tails. During their 30-minute dive, Tom and Kane saw hundreds of species. Back on board the *Poseidon*, Tom told everyone, "It was absolutely incredible!"

oil slick

6

UNDER PRESSURE

Coral reefs are in trouble. They are getting sick. Many are dying. One problem is pollution. Plastic can end up in the ocean, poisoning animals. Oil can cover the water's surface. This prevents sunlight from reaching a reef. Oil can also stick to coral, killing it. Ships that carry goods and tourists sometimes dump their toilets into the ocean. These substances can smother coral reefs.

Other problems include climate change and overfishing. Overfishing is the taking of more fish than can be replaced by the fish's reproduction. Governments can help coral reefs. They can establish marine protected areas. These areas are off limits to commercial fishing. Coral reefs are fragile ecosystems. Humans must make smart choices about how we use the ocean. We must work together to protect the amazing reef creatures that live down in the ocean.

ASK A 🐙 SCIENTIST

What effect does commercial fishing have on coral reefs?

Commercial fisheries provide important sources of food for millions of people living near coral reefs. However, if not managed properly, commercial fisheries can alter the health of the reef. Commercial fisheries typically target large-bodied species of fish because they demand higher prices at the market. Unfortunately, many of these large species are top predators and take a number of years to reach full size. The removal of predatory species like sharks can upset the balance on coral reefs. Also, commercial fisheries often use a variety of fishing techniques that can harm the corals and other organisms. Fishing gear can get tangled or lost and can lead to fish and other reef dwellers getting entangled or trapped.
— Dr. Brian J. Zgliczynski, Marine Ecologist, University of California, San Diego

Disrupting the ecosystem

In the Caribbean Sea, parrotfish and French and gray angel-fish have been overfished. Without these sponge-eating fish, sponge populations have increased. The sponges push out or kill corals. This has hurt many Caribbean reefs.

parrotfish

Largest U.S. marine protected area

In 2006, Papahānaumokuākea (*PA-pa-HA-no-MO-koo-ah-KAY-uh*) Marine National Monument was established in Hawaii. Ten years later, it was expanded. Now it is twice the size of Texas. It is home to more than 7,000 ocean species.

coral bleaching

ASK A 🐙 SCIENTIST

How does climate change affect coral reefs?

Corals are very sensitive to temperature. They will get sick when the water is too warm or too cold. When this happens, a sick coral expels the algae inside it. This is called bleaching. Corals turn bright white without their internal algae. If temperatures return to normal, the algae will come back. The corals will recover. But if bleaching lasts too long, the corals will die. Because of human activities, we are slowly raising the temperature of the oceans. This is putting coral reefs at risk.

— Dr. Andy Shantz, Ocean Researcher, University of California, Santa Barbara

GLOSSARY

adaptations

changes in a species that help it survive in a changed environment

climate change

the gradual increase in Earth's temperature that causes changes in the planet's atmosphere, environments, and long-term weather conditions

commercial

used for business and to gain a profit rather than for personal reasons

crustaceans

animals with no backbone that have a shell covering a soft body

detritus

waste matter, especially from decomposing organisms

DNA

a substance found in every living thing that makes individuals unique

ecosystem

a community of organisms that live together in balance

endangered

at serious risk of dying out completely

evolved

gradually developed into a new form

mangrove

a tree with tangled roots that grows in swampy or coastal areas

species

a group of living beings with shared characteristics and the ability to reproduce with one another

tentacles

slender, flexible limbs in an animal, used for grasping, moving about, or feeling

unpalatable

not pleasant to taste

vertebrate

an animal that has a backbone

SELECTED BIBLIOGRAPHY

Bird, Jonathan. *Secrets of the Reef*. North Reading, Mass.: Jonathan Bird Productions, 2008. DVD, 58 min.

Knowlton, Nancy. *Citizens of the Sea: Wondrous Creatures from the Census of Marine Life*. Washington, D.C.: National Geographic, 2010.

National Oceanic and Atmospheric Administration. "NOAA Coral Reef Conservation Program." https://coralreef.noaa.gov/.

Ocean Portal Team. "Corals and Coral Reefs." Smithsonian National Museum of Natural History. https://ocean.si.edu/corals-and-coral-reefs.

Palumbi, Stephen R., and Anthony R. Palumbi. *The Extreme Life of the Sea*. Princeton, N.J.: Princeton University Press, 2014.

Sheppard, Anne. *Coral Reefs: Secret Cities of the Sea*. London: Natural History Museum, 2015.

INDEX